NOAH'S CAR PARK ARK

Paul Kerensa

Illustrated by Liz and Kate Pope

A long time ago, in a far-off land,

There was just dry sand, and no rain planned.

But a man called Noah, such a wise old fella,

Heard God's voice say, 'Go buy an umbrella!'

find the one
thats

'I'm sending some rain, I think it's for the best,
And I've sent every animal your home address.
No need to panic! It's just two of each,
And you'll float in a boat, till you land on a beach.'

So Noah replied, 'I'll build . . . what? An ark?

A zoo-boat, a petting-ship? A sea-fari park?'

'Exactly!' said God. 'With **hutches** and **hives!**

And room for your wife,

and your sons, and their wives.'

The ark Noah built was really quite big,

A wheel for each hamster, a sty for each pig,

A perch for each parrot, a nest for each mouse,

A kennel, a coop and an elephant house!

His neighbours looked over,

and **grinned** when they heard

That Noah expected each **beast** and each **bird**.

They **laughed** at God's plan (which was not very kind):

'Have a nice cruise!

I think we'll stay behind!'

Soon Noah banged in the last of the nails,

Stood back and looked down . . . to see two tiny snails.

They were crawling on up to the big open doors,

While way in the distance, came two *mighty* ROARS!

Lions and zebras arrived by the pair.

Think of an animal – yup, it was there.

Noah and family looked at the crowd:

It was awfully *smelly* and really quite LOUD!

'Hippos park here . . . insects come next,
Giraffes' feet on ground floor, necks at top decks,
From monkey to donkey, and skylark to *shark*,
They all have a space in my Car Park Ark!'

His sons liked the kennel, his wife loved the hutch,

But space for the rest? There didn't seem much.

'Oh, spaces?' said Noah. 'I've certainly got 'em,

They start at the top, and they fill to the bottom.'

P
ARK

The animals parked up, as if they were cars,

Two **beetles**, two **mustangs** and two **jaguars**.

Last up, the snails finished climbing the ramp,

With shells they'd not noticed were now rather **damp**.

'Quick!', shouted Noah, 'Give the door a good pull!'

And he put up a sign: 'Car Park Ark now **FULL!**'

The floodwaters rose, but the ark stayed afloat.

The animals jiggled within Noah's boat.

CAR PARK
ARK
FULL

It rained and it **rained**, then it **rained** a bit more.

But could it get worse? Yes, **it started to pour!**

Forty days later, blue sky up above,

Noah thought, '*Hmm* . . . I will send out a **dove**.'

Said Mrs Noah, 'Why let the dove fly?'

'Ah!' replied Noah, 'To spy land from the sky!'

So the dove flew away and, when it came back,

It carried a leaf, from a tree, as a snack.

The ark found that tree too –

it *crashed* and it **clattered!**

The mighty doors opened, the animals **scattered.**

And up in the sky, a **rainbow** appeared.

Their **ark-time** was over – the animals **cheered!**

And God made a promise,
to save our creation:
So when we see animals,
birds, vegetation,

Love and respect all
that mooing and barking,
And love this fine space
that God's let us park in.

First published in Great Britain in 2018

Society for Promoting Christian Knowledge
36 Causton Street, London SW1P 4ST
www.spck.org.uk

British Library Cataloguing-in-Publication Data
A catalogue record for this book is available from the British Library

ISBN 978-0-281-07755-7

1 3 5 7 9 10 8 6 4 2

Typeset and designed by Anna Lubecka, Banana Bear Books

Printed in Turkey by Imago

Produced on paper from sustainable forests